# a pirate

Ivan Bulloch & Diane James

**WORLD BOOK / TWO-CAN**

**Art Director:** Ivan Bulloch
**Editor:** Diane James
**Design Assistant:** Lisa Nutt
**Illustrator:** Dom Mansell
**Photographer:** Daniel Pangbourne
**Models:** Kaz, Jonathan, Alicia, Grant, Courtney, Abi
**Special thanks to:** Karen Ingebretsen, World Book Publishing

**Adult assistance may be necessary for some of the activities in this book.**

First published in the United States and Canada in 1997 by
World Book, Inc.
525 W. Monroe
Chicago, IL 60661
in association with Two-Can Publishing Ltd.

© Two-Can Publishing Ltd., 1997

**For information on other World Book products,
call 1-800-255-1750, x 2238.**

ISBN: 0-7166-5506-3 (hard cover)
ISBN: 0-7166-5507-1 (soft cover)
LC: 96-61756

Printed in Spain

1 2 3 4 5 6 7 8 9 10 01 00 99 98 97

# Contents

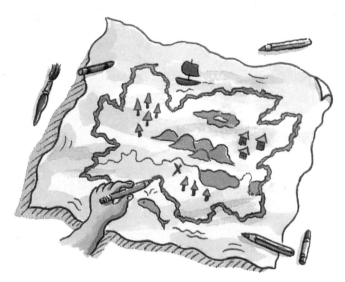

4...Once Upon a Time!

6...Getting Dressed

glue

glue

18...A Very Old Map

20...Pirate Biscuits

22...Attack!

8...The Captain's Hat

10...Swords and Daggers

12...Ship Ahoy!

14...Life on Board

16...Buried Treasure

24...Chit Chat!

Pirates were fierce and brave sea robbers. They sailed the seas in search of merchant ships full of riches. After a noisy battle, the pirates tied up their prisoners and grabbed all the valuables on board. If you would like to be a pirate, you'll need to prepare before setting off on your adventures. *So let's begin...*

On the whole, pirates were a scruffy bunch. They wore the same pants and shirts for days on end! Because they were always fighting at sea, their clothes soon got ragged and extremely smelly!

Sometimes pirates used scarves to keep their messy hair tied back and also to keep their pants from falling down!

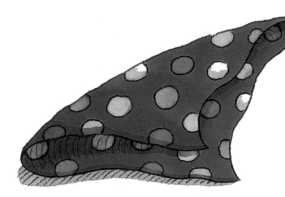

**1** Find a large scarf or square shape of material and fold it in half diagonally. Well done, that was the easy part!

**2** Hold one end in each hand and pull the long edge tight across your forehead. Pull the ends around to the back and tie a knot.

*I'm ready for anything!*

**3** For a different scarf, fold a square of material over and over to make a long strip. Wind it around your head and tie a knot.

**4** To finish your outfit, find an old T-shirt and cut a jagged edge along the bottom. Tie some lengths of rope around the legs of your pants.

7

**S**pecial pirates, like the captain, wore a hat to show how brave and important they were. Very well-known pirates had their own special scary badges that they wore on their hats.

**1** To make your own pirate's hat, measure your head with a tape measure. Use the measurement to cut out two shapes, like the ones below, from thick black paper. Glue them together at the sides.

glue

glue

Few pirates managed to escape getting injured in battle. That's why so many pirates wore a black patch over one eye!

**2** Cut some shapes from white paper to make a badge. You could make a scary skull and crossbones! Glue your badge pieces to the front of your hat.

**Who does he think he's scaring?**

**3** Cut a shape like the one above from black paper to make your pirate's eye-patch. Make a hole at either side and thread through a length of string. Tie the string around your head.

**Don't mess with Captain Tom!**

No pirate felt safe without a weapon! He used a sword and dagger for hand-to-hand fighting and a gun for shooting. The captain made his crew sharpen and polish their weapons every day until they sparkled!

Two swords are better than one!

**1** Cut a sword or dagger shape from thick cardboard. Corrugated cardboard is best because it is thick, but not too difficult to cut.

**2** Paint the blade and handle of your sword. Wind some thick string around the handle to give you a better grip.

11

irates needed to be able to see ships that were far, far away. A tiny spot on the horizon might be a ship full of riches – just perfect for a pirate raid! The best way to find out was by using a powerful telescope that made everything look very close.

*Faster!*

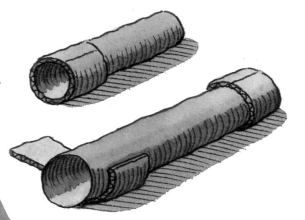

**2** Wind a cardboard strip around each end of the long tube and one end of the short tube. Glue them down.

Ship ahoy! Look lively.

**1** Find two cardboard rolls. One should be small enough to fit inside the other. The small roll will be the eyepiece for the telescope and should be about half the length of the larger roll. Cut three strips from corrugated cardboard to fit around the ends of the tubes.

**3** Push the smaller tube a short way into the longer one and paint all of the pieces – black for the main parts and gold or yellow for the brass end pieces.

**P**irate ships had to be strong and reliable. Huge sails helped speed them along. Life on board was pretty uncomfortable! There wasn't much room to move, and it was often cold and damp!

**1** Find a big, strong cardboard box. Cut off 3 of the flaps, leaving one short flap to make the "prow." Shape it into a triangle.

The flag waving from the top of the mast warned people off – a small red flag meant "Prepare to Die!"

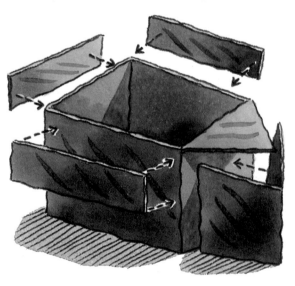

**2** Glue the flaps to the sides and back of the box to look like planks. Cut a strip of cardboard the same height as the box and wide enough to fold in half and glue or tape to the prow and sides of the boat.

Look out, here I come!

**3** Paint the background color for your boat. Before it dries, paint on swirly stripes and rings to make the cardboard look like wood.

**4** Use a sturdy tree branch or an old broom handle for the mast. Cut a piece of material with 2 ties and attach it to the end of the mast as shown above.

After a raid, pirates often had to find a safe place to hide their treasure. They had to make sure nobody could steal it before they could get back to retrieve it!

$\frac{1}{3}$

$\frac{2}{3}$

**1** A large cardboard box makes a good treasure chest. Tape up the ends and cut around 3 sides – leaving one long side for the hinge.

The best hiding place was in a strong, wooden chest with a lock. The chest was buried as deep as a pirate could possibly dig!

**2** Decorate your chest with colored paper and foil-covered chocolate coins. Don't forget a lock and key! Make holes in each of the short ends and poke some rope through to make handles. Now fill your chest with your favorite treasures.

Generally speaking, pirates didn't have good memories. So it was important to make a map to show where they had buried their treasure. It might be a very long time before they could return to dig it up! The worst thing that could possibly happen was for the map to fall into enemy hands!

**1** Take a sheet of plain white paper. Soak a teabag in some water and squeeze out most of the water. Wipe it over the surface of the paper to make it look old.

*Don't tell anyone else where the treasure is!*

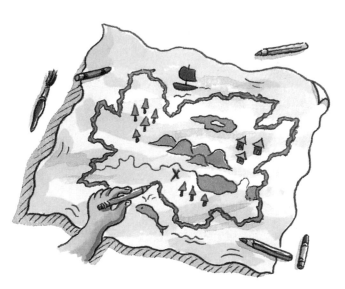

**2** When the paper is dry, draw the outline of your map. Sketch rivers, trees, hills, and villages – anything that might help to pinpoint exactly where the treasure is buried!

**3** Finally, draw an X to mark the treasure. Crumple up the map to make it look even more old and wrinkled. Keep it in a secret place!

It wasn't often that you came across a healthy pirate! There were no vegetables or fresh fruit on board. For weeks on end pirates had to make do with salted food and dry biscuits.

*Who's been nibbling my biscuit?*

What little food they had was shared with the ship's rats and weevils – UGH!

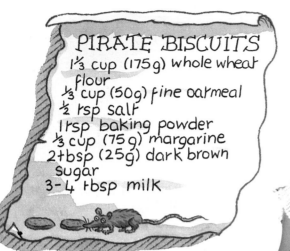

PIRATE BISCUITS
1⅓ cup (175g) whole wheat flour
⅓ cup (50g) fine oatmeal
½ tsp salt
1 tsp baking powder
⅓ cup (75g) margarine
2 tbsp (25g) dark brown sugar
3-4 tbsp milk

**1** Make pirate biscuits! Mix together the flour, oatmeal, salt, baking powder, and sugar. Use a fork to mix in the margarine until the mixture looks like breadcrumbs.

**2** Pour the milk in and mix to a firm dough.

**3** Put the dough on a floured surface and roll it out about a quarter inch (1cm) thick. Use a small glass to cut out circles of dough.

**4** Put the biscuits on a greased cookie sheet or baking pan. Bake them at 375° F. (190° C) for 15 to 20 minutes. When they are cool, you can enjoy a delicious pirate snack!

An attack by a pirate ship was a scary event! The pirates drew alongside a ship and threw hooks and ropes over to keep the two ships together. Then they leapt aboard, brandishing swords, daggers, and pistols and making as much noise as possible! This was enough to make most people surrender immediately – before a single drop of blood was spilled.

*A pirate's life was never, ever dull!*

Looks like we're winning!

**P**irates sometimes used words that would sound very strange today! Here are just a few to help you carry on a pirate conversation.

*You lily-livered scaredy-cat.*

*You're just a coward.*

*Ahoy there, me hearties!*

*Hi, how are you?*

*Seize my soul if I give you quarter.*

*You're not getting anything from me.*

*Scurvy knave!*

*Dirty rat!*

*Shiver me timbers!*

*What a surprise!*